Footplate Tales
of the
Settle-Carlisle Railway

A Revised Edition

August, 1986. 5305 takes water from the tanker on the overbridge at Long Preston. The driver takes a quick look around the locomotive.

Footplate Tales of the Settle-Carlisle Railway

Text: W. R. Mitchell

Visuals: Peter Fox

CASTLEBERG

Some of the men who drove and "fired" the steam locomotives on the 72-mile-long route over the stormy Pennines tell of their experiences.

Ex-LMS "Duchess of Hamilton"
at Blea Moor, 1983

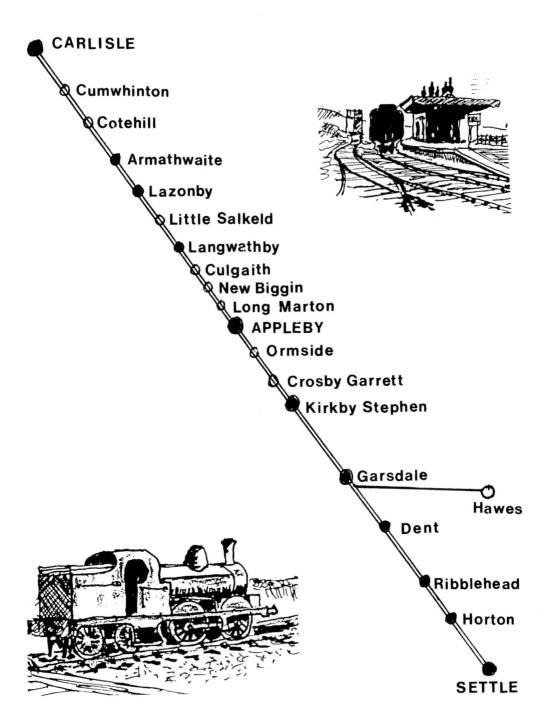

CARLISLE
Cumwhinton
Cotehill
Armathwaite
Lazonby
Little Salkeld
Langwathby
Culgaith
New Biggin
Long Marton
APPLEBY
Ormside
Crosby Garrett
Kirkby Stephen
Garsdale — Hawes
Dent
Ribblehead
Horton
SETTLE

Typeset and printed by Lamberts Print & Design, Station Road, Settle, North Yorkshire, BD24 9AA.
Published by W.R. Mitchell, 18 Yealand Avenue, Giggleswick, Settle, North Yorkshire, BD24 0AY.
© Text, W.R. Mitchell, 1989. Revised edition 2004.
ISBN: 1 871064 07 4

Contents

Illustrations:

Front cover, top – The driver of an Ex-LMS Stanier Class 5. *Left* – A spell with the oil can. *Below* – Stanier Class 5 storms the Drag.

Back cover, top – The last steam locomotive to be built for BR No.92220 "Evening Star" climbs to Aisgill summit in fine style with the crew obviously hard at work, judging by the claggy black smoke. *Bottom* – The crew of the Stanier Black Five No.44871 take a breather at Settle Junction whilst waiting for the signalman to give them the road for a journey to Carlisle. (Peter Fox).

This page, above – BR driver Radcliffe at the controls of Jubilee 5596 "Bahamas".

Peter Fox – All uncredited drawings and photographs.

W R Mitchell – 11 (bottom), 12 (bottom), 13, 16, 19, 27, 33 (bottom), 41 (top), 42 (top).

Richard Bancroft – 1, 18.

Acknowledgements

Special thanks to Cyril Patrickson, W C Addy, Jimmy Fishwick, Fred Jarvis and many other footplate men.

Foreword

by

Driver Cyril Patrickson

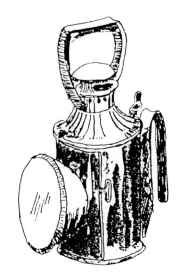

I NEED little encouragement to talk or write about the Settle-Carlisle line, which I have known – as firemen and driver – for 40 years. I retired from railway service in April, 1991. I want to be on the Carlisle line as often as possible.

My first experience of storming The Drag from Settle to Aisgill was in December, 1949, when I arrived in Skipton as a fireman. I had already heard many tales of the famous railway. I was born into a railway family.

Grandfather, William Patrickson, started his career as a porter at Appleby and became a goods guard at Carlisle. My father, who was also christened William, was born at Appleby and became a passenger guard at Bradford (Forster Square), from which, each weekday, the express known as Bonnyface set off on its exciting journey to Garsdale and Hawes. My brother and I began work on the railway when we left school.

I experienced the last days of Steam and the dawning of the Age of the Diesel. When volunteers were requested to drive "steam specials," I was happy to respond. Now I took command of some of the best-known locomotives in the land. I drove the *Flying Scotsman* from Hellifield to Settle on Centenary Day in 1976. I was in charge of the Evening Star which Eric Treacy (The Railway Bishop) was photographing at Appleby on the day he died; and I drove that self-same locomotive to the memorial service, held at Appleby and attended by thousands.

Years ago, firing or driving a steam locomotive was a dirty, hard job. I would not have missed it for anything. It was the challenge of a ruling gradient of 1 in 100 that appealed.

I am glad that some of the tales of drivers and firemen have been noted in book form. They will surely give pleasure to the Settle-Carlisle fans of today and those yet unborn. For we hope that the line will survive for many years to come.

Water tank at Blea Moor.

An Introduction

Portrait of a "Crab", ex-LMS freight engine used on Settle-Carlisle from 1930s to 1960s.

MY GODFATHER, Ted Boak, was a driver on the Settle-Carlisle. He told of thrashing steam engines between Settle and the summit at Aisgill; of being in the second engine, drenched by disturbed snow, when drifts were being cleared on the Wensleydale line; and of approaching Ribblehead viaduct in a gale, when he and the fireman – having seen that the firebox was glowing satisfactorily – crouched in sheltered corners of the cab and let the locomotive take care of itself as the wind howled about them.

Ted Boak also mentioned when a platelayer at Garsdale cadged some coal for the lineside hut. It was delivered with great precision. At Garsdale, an enormous cob of coal was balanced on the edge of the tender, to be dropped at what was judged to be the right moment. Like the celebrated "bouncing" bomb of the Second World War, the coal travelled far. It crashed through the door of the platelayers' hut, scattering the occupants.

This book is mainly about the Steam Age. The drivers and firemen varied in size and temperament but were bound together by the spirited response that was needed to operate trains along the 72-mile long railway that linked North Ribblesdale with the Eden Valley via the high Pennine hills.

Some footplate men were native born and spoke local dialect. One man, asked for the time of day, said: "Yen (one) o'clock, young feller, me lad." Not all the drivers appreciated the special beauty of the high dale country. A fireman was extolling the pleasures of Mallerstang in the spring. The driver, who hailed from Wakefield, simply replied: "Your grass is no greener than t'stuff we've got in Wek'field."

Family pride was detectable. A driver remarked: "My mother had three of us on t'railway. We were on different shifts, so t'table were never cleared of food. Mother had three lots of packing up. Sandwiches, of course!"

The Settle-Carlisle was being built between 1869 and 1875, when freight traffic was introduced to consolidate the track. On May 1, 1876, the line was opened for passenger traffic. The precise length of the railway, from Settle

Junction to Petteril Bridge Junction, is 72 miles 1,728 yards, with a further 6 miles 132 yards for the branch from Garsdale to Hawes.

Two-thirds of the Settle-Carlisle are in Cumbria. Over 20 miles of line have a gradient of 1 in 100 and, quite apart from the celebrated Long Drag, from Settle to Aisgill, there is a wearying Drag from Appleby to Aisgill for traffic going south. Many a perspiring fireman has been so elated by the sight of the "distant" signal for Aisgill that it became known as the Star of Bethlehem.

When the northward bound train left Appleby, there was a respite for the footplate men. "After you got through Long Meg, you started getting your fire warmed up again because you were going to go up Lazonby Bank. You had to run at it. When you got through Baron Wood tunnels, you could ease back again for the gentle dip to Low House and the road crossing." The footplate men were pleased to see Carlisle after the 72 miles of hard going from Settle Junction. "You were tired. You knew that you could have an hour or two and get some food and drink."

The men were equal to all emergencies. A goods train from Carlisle to Skipton arrived at Blea Moor on a dark, windy night. The crew heard the signalman call out: "Operation Midwife." The firemen went to investigate. "At that time, platelayers lived in the cottages near Blea Moor box. One of the wives was expecting a baby and was getting towards the end of her time.

"We had to transport her from Blea Moor on an old Derby 4. We had 48 goods wagons on t'back on us. We drove down to Ribblehead. Joe Shepherd was the Stationmaster then. His wife was waiting for us. She had a mop cap and was wearing an old raincoat. Joe stood with his waterproofs and his oil lamp. The ambulance was waiting. We got her into the ambulance and off she went to have her baby."

In the old days, the "mighty Midland" had very small locomotives. As the weight of the trains increased, they had to work them double-headed. The Derby 4 had about 180lb boiler pressure. Larger engines, such as the Black 5s, and the Class 8 freights, had a bigger firebox and grate area and a 225lb boiler pressure.

Coal and water composed the staple diet, but during the 1939-45, the fuel came in the form of brickettes. A fireman told me: "They were like tennis balls. Awful things! If you'd a tender full of them they were always rolling off the footplate. We used to like to go to Holbeck and get big cobs of coal; then we could put them in the back corners and wall it up. Hence the expression: 'Walling your back corners up...' "

One tale that is re-told with gusto dates from the 1939-45 war, when some of the signal boxes on the Settle-Carlisle were operated by women. A driver had been accustomed to going into a box and saying to the signalman – "Come on: get 'em off!" He was referring to the pegs. "You wanted to be going, particularly if you were on mileage work." A Leeds fireman was said to have gone into a box on the Drag and remarked: "Come on – get 'em off!" The lady signaller thought he meant something else. She slapped his face and reported him!

Ex SR 777, Sir Lamiel, coasting south at Ribblehead.

Learning
the Job

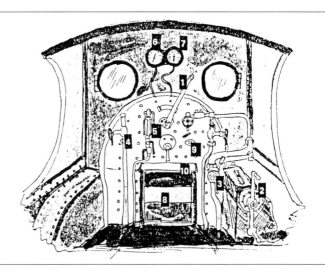

A simplified drawing of a Midland locomotive cab. 1) Steam regulator. 2) Screw reversing handle. 3) Vacuum brake. 4) Injector (water to boiler). 5) Water gauge. 6) Vacuum brake pressure gauge. 7) Steam pressure gauge. 8) Firebox doors. 9) Registered working pressure plate. 10) Drip tray.

ALMOST every boy wanted to be an engine-driver. The lowest rung of the ladder leading to this exalted position was occupied by the cleaner. All the menial tasks in a Shed were given to the new-starter who, with cotton waste and mineral oil, was set to work clambering into the "motions" of the locomotive. "The senior cleaner made sure he had a nice job, such as dealing with the tanks or walking about on the boiler."

A man who began his railway career at Hellifield, first working for Lanky (Lancashire and Yorkshire Railway) and then, from January, 1922, for the Midland Railway, went through the classic routine of cleaner, fireman and driver. As a cleaner, aged 17, he worked a shift system. "The shifts began at 7.30am, 2.30pm and 11 pm. Apart from cleaning, a lad also assisted the 'coalman' with 'coaling engines'. We didn't get any extra pay for it. A labourer got about £2.2s a week; we were getting 30s a week."

On the coal stage at Hellifield, in the Lanky days, "the system was not like the 'Midland' where you filled them and weighed them and tipped them. The coal was put in large boxes and two of you had to wind these boxes up on a crane. Then you swung the boom of the crane round and tipped the coal on to the tender. It wasn't easy. A box on a crane was not something stationary. It could move about. One box pushed Isaac Hailwood off the tender. He was off work quite a bit..."

Under this routine, engines were "called up" to receive attention. "You had different types of engine – passenger and goods, for instance – and they had different classes of coal. We called the inferior type 'legs and arms'. It was from Wharncliffe and was right long stuff, as brittle as you could make it. Then we had Wigan coal. There was a lot of heat in it but it ran a lot and 'soldered' the bars up. It wasn't very good. You had to put a lot of limestone or brick on to the fire when you got Wigan coal. The best stuff, Yorkshire Main coal, was kept for the passenger trains..."

A Skipton driver now close to retirement recalls leaving school at 14 years old. "I had to go to Carrs the grocers for a year so that I could qualify to take up employment on the railway. That grocery job brought me 12s.6d a week. I became a boy porter in 1941 and got 12s.6d a week."

At the larger Sheds, a cleaner was introduced to a shift system. The youngest began work at 7.30am. The railway wanted a cheap labour system; it allowed older men to do some labouring and paid them the mean rate between cleaner and labourer. Starting work, the cleaner collected from the Stores the waste and oil he needed. "By cleaning a locomotive, he became familiar with all the working parts – the side-rods, big-ends, tender, boiler…"

The end result of some years of dedication was a new status – that of passed cleaner. "It was another cut-price job. You took a 'firing examination', if required, you went out as a fireman. Otherwise you were stuck in the Shed as a cleaner. You had to have a little knowledge about the workings of a locomotive and about rules and regulations."

At Skipton, at one time, a shortage of firemen caused problems. "The blokes they used were comparatively young and sometimes they were not too familiar with the Settle-Carlisle. There was a young lad who'd come from York. He wasn't keeping a big enough fire. The driver drew his attention to the tall chimney at the Hoffman kiln at Langcliffe and said that the summit of the line was about level with the top. The lad nearly broke his neck looking up at the chimney. Then he started shovelling like mad!"

A fireman, reporting for duty, signed on, familiarised himself with the latest notices about the line, and looked at the big engine board which gave details of the engines to be used, the roads to be followed and the type of work to be done. "You went to your locomotive, put your coat and food in the locker and then went to the stores for a bucket, spanners, lamps and coal pick."

The fireman then prepared his fire, which during the night had been kept "under the door" – or in the back corners of the box. "Otherwise it would be blowing steam off all night… The fireman had to pull a bit out, and put a bit on, and gradually build up the fire till the steam began to rise."

The fireman who aspired to be a driver took the required examination and became a passed fireman; he did driver's duties as required. "You couldn't tell t'railway company owt about saving brass. They didn't spend a penny if they

could think of a way of saving it… For a time they got a cut-price fireman and a cut-price driver."

Reporting for duty, the driver oiled the side rods and checked the moving parts. "In the case of a freight train, bound for Carlisle and Scotland, it might be coke for Rutherglen, wagons full of potatoes or other sorts of merchandise... You backed on to your train, the guard told you the tonnage – and away you went."

A man was approached by a fellow driver who wanted to know how he managed to get up so promptly to go on duty. "I told him: 'Well – I hev to go to bed to get up, that's all'. He said: 'How do you go on about beer?' I said: 'I don't. If I have a lot o'beer I can't wakken up at t'time 'at I say'.

"He said: 'Hey you seen them clocks they've just brought out'. I said: 'No'. He said: 'I've a catalogue somewhere; I'll fetch it tomorrow'. It was a clock called Moonbeams. I bought a heck of a lot for people who couldn't get up.

"I bought one for a chap who had to be wakkened up by his mother. A few minutes after, she'd go back into his bedroom and he'd be fast asleep again. She just took bedclothes off and slung 'em on to t'floor. Left him wi' nowt except pyjamas. And then she'd go back again and find he'd followed t'blankets on to t'floor and was curled up. She had to use water on 'im… – Well, when he were gettin' wed, I bowt him one o' them clocks. It never failed, so he said. It's my firm belief that if one o' them Westclox Moonbeams was set for 3am, and put outside o' t'cemetery gates, they'd all get up and walk. I bowt one. I could then get a bit more beer down me."

Opposite page –   ➤
Above: Midland Compound 100 at Hawes Junction (now known as Garsdale) in Edwardian days. From a painting by Alan Fearnley.
Below: Two Johnson 4-4-0s at Hellifield, c1905. (W R Mitchell collection).

Signal Service

Left – The old box on Blea Moor stood beside the down-line.

Left, below – Neville Cagill in the present Blea Moor box.

Right – The late, lamented Aisgill box, now preserved at Butterley, Derbyshire.

Right, below – Derek Soames cooks a kipper in the box at Settle Junction.

Permission had been given for the photographer to enter the boxes.

A Driver's Life

5XP

FIRE, boiling water, steam – this is the process at work in a locomotive. Steam rises to work the valves, which are connected through rods and big-ends to the wheels. Basically, coal is burnt in a firebox. The fire gives off gases which pass through tubes surrounded by water. The heated water becomes steam, which rises to the top of the locomotive and to the regulator valve, under its distinctive dome. Injectors transfer water from the tender to the boiler and there are gauge glasses to enable the footplate men to check on the amount of water in reserve.

A driver who had a reputation for speed on the rails never did more than 30 miles an hour when driving his car. "I couldn't go fast enough on an engine." Another driver – "gentleman through and through" – was an exceedingly fine engineman. "When he'd set the regulator, you would have an easy trip on any job. He would never alter that regulator. He would hardly ever sit down. His overalls were spotlessly clean, with a crease down them. He used to enjoy visiting Carlisle for the dialect. He would sit there and quietly mention the place of origin of any man who was talking. 'That chap's from Glasgow', he would say. You got all the Scottish dialects in the Barracks at Carlisle. His brother, who was also on the railway, was quite different. He didn't keep himself tidy and he was usually as black as the ace of spades!"

A good driver was considerate to his fireman. When Jimmy Fishwick became a driver, he was told by a man he greatly respected: "Now, Jim, when you get driving, remember that if you are going to pass Lazonby in the time that's in the time book, 19 minutes, you will be knocking it out of your fireman. I always lose about five minutes to Low House. Now the Midland (Carlisle) men don't; they want to pass Low House in 13 minutes."

On a steam locomotive, the men used a special railway language. "To stop, nobody ever said 'stop' – a driver or fireman would shout 'whoa'. That was the word that everybody would re-act to, Shout whooooa – and bang goes the brake!"

The Black Five was considered "a good engine." It was a dual purpose engine, good for passenger or freight work. "It would take 53 wagons to Carlisle." A Hellifield driver, thinking about the Black Fives, recalled with special pleasure a 6B engine. "You got on a 6B engine and you never had any problems at all."

A driver had 15 bogies (456 tons) on his train one day. He should have had only 390 tons. "The so-called pilot from Kingmoor was riding in the train with the passengers. I was pressing on, keeping my own timings, and he frightened half the passengers to death by telling them I was going too fast. When I was relieved at Hellifield, the stationmaster said I was in trouble. 'The passengers are complaining that you were going too fast'. I met the pilot in the mess-room and told him off quietly. I said 'I would have been better without him'."

The fireman had to keep his eye on the signals, for the driver was not expected to cross the cab to look for them. Yet when he passed his examination as a driver, he was told never to accept the fireman's word that a signal was clear. "Signals were never placed as they are these days so that they can be seen easily. An old semaphore signal could be in somebody's backyard, high up on a post or round the corner! And, boy, when you were working on Carlisle 'road', you were looking all over the place… Coming from Carlisle you were always pleased to see the Star of Bethlehem, that 'distant' signal for Aisgill. As soon as you spotted that, you knew the hard climbing was nearly over…"

I asked a grizzle-grey driver: "Have you ever been stuck for steam?"

Laughter. "I've stuck for steam more times than thou has hair on thi 'eeard. Some fellers are numbskulls. Best time was when I had twelve month with a driver who'd been in t'first world war. When he came back, he was put in t'front of all them that had been made drivers while he had been away. We took days about. He fired one day, I fired the next. The way he worked, I worked. We never stuck once.

"But I've been stuck at every signal between South Junction and Delaney's and Aisgill. We only just clanked ower at Low House. And with between 60 and 80 pounds, neither of the injectors worked."

The loose-coupled goods train is now but a faint memory. Nearly every goods train on the Drag was loose-coupled. It called for a lot of experience and skill to keep the couplings tight. A driver benefited from the guard's knowledge of the "road." The guard applied the hand-brake of his van when going downhill. "It was said that some guards had a match box. They put some marbles in and they had it on the seat beside them. When the marbles moved to the far end of the box, the train was going downhill. If they came towards him, the train was going uphill! He then put his brake on or off, whichever way he wanted." In the days of loose-coupled trains, it was possible to see the wheels of a guard's

No.5305 storms past Helwith Bridge with a northbound "Pennine Limited", July, 1986.

van when the train was on a steep downward gradient; they were sparkling like Catherine wheels in the darkness as the guard kept the handbrake on to ensure the couplings were tight.

Some drivers did not like certain guards. "They were either reading a book or nodding off... You could brake the engine and put a shake on. That gave the guard a bit of a reminder to keep his mind on his job!" The driver of a passenger train with an attendant dining car was blamed for any breakages, whether or not he had an abrupt action while driving.

Bonnyface, the Bradford-Hawes express was popular with drivers, one of whom recalls walking up the market town and buying a baby Wensleydale cheese at the Creamery for 3s.9d. "I used to bring a cheese home in late autumn and we kept it in the pantry until Christmas."

I met a retired driver who pointed to one of his eyes and said: "I've a piece o' coal in. It'll be there when I dee. I might leave it to one o' them." He pointed to his family. They were not amused.

Jimmy Fishwick, of Hellifield, one of the drivers on The Drag.

Shovelling to Carlisle

"WHAT was it like being a fireman up the Drag?" I asked a veteran.

"What was it like? Very enjoyable." He laughed immoderately.

"How much coal did you use?"

"How would I know? Some firemen were good; some were 'very light'. Some of them knew how to use the machinery; others didn't even even know if it were raining or not. They'd have been grossly overpaid if they were paid with holes out of washers. I can't put it no plainer than that... If the fireman was a rough feller, he could use owt up to four ton between Skipton and Carlisle. A feller what were sensible wouldn't reach three ton."

The fireman continued: "Also – and don't forget this – I for one used to give a hell of a lot of coal away. I never brok owt up what wouldn't go in t'hole. If it were too big to go in t'hole, it went over t'side. Platelayers or anyone else who cared about it could have it. There was a garden near t'railway. I used to pop big pieces into a bloke's garden, in among his bushes. He didn't mind as long as they were not near his greenhouse. When I retired, I bet he missed me aw reight."

Above – A Midland Railway 2F 0-6-0 with half-cab and very little weather protection.

Below – In contrast, a Midland Railway 3F 0-6-0, which had an extended cab and therefore more protection. Both locomotive types were well liked by the footplatemen.

I also heard of the old lady with a lineside garden who placed a row of empty bottles on the wall. No self-respecting fireman could resist throwing cobs of coal at the bottles. The old lady was assured of having plenty of fuel.

Every type of steam engine was fired in a different manner. The fire had to be built according to the shape of the firebox. "A good fireman sat with his eyes glued on the chimney top. There should be just a haze; if there was black smoke, the fire was not burning properly. As soon as the haze cleared, the fire was ready for some more coal. If you did not put some on within minutes, then the steam pressure came down. As the fire became dirtier, the fireman worked harder. He kept his eye on the chimney top. If the blast was constant, he 'fired' regular away. Seven shovelfuls. Three down either side. One under the door.

"If it was a freight train, with lumps and a lot of dust, you rested the blade of the shovel on the firebox mouthpiece and the blast would take it. If you had a lot of slack, you kept the bottom door up, the top flat open and you dribbled coal in. You let it take it where it wanted. That also mucked your tubes up."

The "firing shovel" was a long-bladed shovel, rounded at the back so that coal wouldn't slip off. An even more impressive shovel – the "clinker shovel" or paddle – had a shaft from five to six feet long. This shovel was used for cleaning the ashes from the firebox. "Before they allowed you to take the bars up, and push the clinkers and the fire into the ash pan, you had to use a 'paddle'."

A fireman at a time when Class 3s (0-6-0) were stabled at Hellifield recalled the extra protection from the weather. He had worked on the L and Y Railway, when "there was just something over top of your head, so to speak... The seat was made of iron and you had to get yourself a bit of wood" With the Midland, you had good shelter and a proper box to sit on."

On the demanding Settle-Carlisle, a driver regarded any new fireman with suspicion, sometimes with resentment. A Leeds man, recalling his first trip, says: "The driver was boss on the footplate; it was important to get on with him. This one was a boozing pal of my dad's but it made no difference to his attitude towards me.

"I kept the engine going, with steam to spare, all the way up the Drag. The driver actually smiled. As we were crossing Denthead viaduct, with the driver leaning out of the cab to look for signals, the wind coming down the valley caught hold of me and but for a handle I grabbed, I would have been blown off the footplate. On the way back, the driver gave me an orange at Garsdale!"

Sometimes a driver would lend a hand with "firing." He'd say: "Come out o' t'rooad. Give us 'od." And he would put a few shovelfuls of coal on the fire. "The Compound firebox was eleven foot. You

The driver of a pick-up train.

were throwing coal eleven foot through a narrow hole. If you missed a place on a steam engine, when it was working heavily, the steam (pressure) would come down almost immediately. You got no smoke and the fire would burn unevenly. 'Tha's missed some'. So you opened the door and started again till you got the right place. It really was a skilful job."

Not many firemen could claim to have worked between Leeds and Carlisle without "sticking." Sometimes, a steam train on the Drag ran out of steam. "In all the years I was on, this never happened on the Settle side, but coming back it happened twice. Let's face it, if it was pouring down and you were shovelling water into a firebox, you'd come to a standstill."

Carlisle Kingmoor, in the 1930s, when a Leeds man became a fireman on the Drag, was an extremely busy place. "You 'booked off' and went to your lodgings for the offduty spell. You left your engine in the 'engine line'. It was moved in stages to the 'ash pit'. There were two rows, with as many as 20 or 30 engines, waiting to have their fires cleaned. Men were cleaning full-time. It was an hour's job to do one engine."

A visiting fireman recalls walking down to the Shed at Carlisle and discovering with surprise that some of the cleaners and "putback firemen" were older than his dad. "The cleaning rate was 36s a week. If you were firing, you got 57s. When you got put-back, you were put-back in rate as well. I was firing. I was getting fireman's rate. I felt sorry for some of the others who'd slipped back."

A fireman had time to build up his fire when the train was at the southern approaches to the Settle-Carlisle. From Skipton, there is a gradual climb to Delaney's, and from Delaney's the way is a gentle incline through Gargrave and Bell Busk. At Hellifield, the steam can be cut off. "The train would coast down to Settle Junction."

In Steam Time, a fireman's eyes were upon the "distant" signal. "It could be seen from the fireman's side. If it was green, you said to the driver: 'It's all off'. And then you got stuck in. You'd be firing all the time. You gave it more regulator. How hard the fireman worked depended on the type of locomotive, and how big a load you had. If he was 'firing' a Jubilee, hauling an express, he was working. Because of the beat, a Jubilee put it up into the atmosphere quicker than you could put it into the firebox."

A fireman built up the fire before reaching Blea Moor tunnel; he did not want to have to replenish it as the locomotive ran through 2,629 yards of darkness. "If the wind was the wrong way – for you! – and you were slipping a lot, all the exhaust gases came back into the cab, with a choking effect for the crew."

After the hard work on the Drag, the summit of the line was reached at Aisgill. "Then the driver was telling me to have my sandwiches and tea because we could free-wheel down to Kirkby Stephen. By the time we got to Appleby, we would be starting into it again on Lazonby Bank... Sometimes we changed over at Appleby. That was hard going because you had climbed all the way up the Drag, you'd dropped down the other side and when you'd been relieved by the Carlisle men at Appleby, you had to climb all the way back!"

A southbound train more often than not had a following wind. "It could be a cold wind. I've fired engines wearing my heavy railway mac. The heat of the fire was fantastic. My overalls were being scorched at one side and ice was forming on the bucket eight feet away."

Rain washed the muck from the tender. "It was never the cobs of coal – just the muck. The slurry. I've known days so wet that t'driver had to help out; he opened and shut t'firebox door after every shovelful. We had to keep yon fire warm!"

46229 – Duchess of Hamilton – leaves Ribblehead in a strong easterly wind, August, 1984.

Coal and Water

An artist's impression of an early Midland Railway 2-4-0 passenger locomotive taking water. No.817 was a regular visitor to the Settle-Carlisle.

PASSENGER TRAINS leaving Holbeck Shed and Carlisle Shed were supplied with coal of a much higher quality than that used in freight work. In each case, the coal came from Manvers Main. It was the sort of hard, brittle "steam coal" that in careless hands produced "baby oranges", blazing lumps of half-burnt material emanating from the chimney. If a fireman was not correctly regulating his fire, and had all the dampers open, the blast took the small coal across the fire. It was still burning when it was blown clear of the locomotive.

Cheap coal for freight locomotives, which came from a "day hole" in the Dearne Valley, was "long, thin, crumbly stuff." Sometimes a sliver from a piece being shovelled into "t'fire hole" slid back and lacerated the hand of the fireman.

A man, who drove with consideration might burn three tons on a specific journey, whereas another, who was wasteful, needed three and a half or even four tons for the same distance. It was vital, on some freight jobs, for the tender to be full. The capacity could be increased by arranging long cobs of coal like a wall around the top of the tender and packing more coal behind the wall. In this way, the crew might manage to take aboard an extra two tons. It was known for a freight locomotive to be so heavily laden with coal that it could hardly scrape through the door of the Shed.

One driver who was "only about t'size of two pennorth o' copper," and who perched rather than sat on his seat, was known to yank the regulator open instead of handling it sensitively. He usually "scorched" the rail as he started. When the locomotive was moving, he put the regulator straight over. The fireman was in perpetual motion keeping up with the demand for steam.

The platelayers, at their wooden hut by the track, had a coal allocation, but it was rarely sufficient for their needs. Consequently, one of the men would use sign language and shout to invite the crew of a train to leave some as they passed. "The platelayers would hold their hands together, with fingers stretched out, forming a square that represented a cob of coal. If we were 'inside' at Garsdale, one chap turned up with a wheelbarrow. He wanted us to fill it with coal."

A driver was passing Helwith Bridge, where the platelayers' cabin is at the bottom of a bank, when he saw a platelayer shouting and waving his arms. He wanted a large cob of coal. "In those days we got big, hard cobs from a Yorkshire colliery. I picked a huge piece and threw it. But it bounced straight down to the cabin and knocked the door open."

In 1947, a year remembered for its heavy snowfalls, a crew signed on to work the 5.45pm out of Skipton. "It started to snow. I'd only half a tank o' watter, enough to take me to Blea Moor, where I could fill up. And that were that! It didn't happen that way. They stopped me at Ribblehead. A Leeds man was coming up behind. They said: 'He hasn't any watter', I said: 'Neither have I, owd lad'. I was told: 'It saves a block' I said: 'I'm not bothered about what it's going to save. In t'long run, it's going to lose'. They said: 'Well you ain't going till he comes'. That was that."

If, for some reason, a locomotive ran out of water, the fireman had to feverishly throw out the fire. 'This happened to us at Helwith Bridge. We were working a 'fitted' to Carlisle; we ran short of water. The gauge was faulty. Somebody had prepared the locomotive on the Shed. When we passed Settle, we had a full gauge. We should have had nearly a full tender of water. But we hadn't! As I was coming up by the Craven Quarry, I put my injector on and there was no water. It was dry and I had a firebox full of red-hot fire.

"The next water column was at Blea Moor. We asked the signalman to clear the main line, then backed inside at Foredale, which we shouldn't have done, really, because it was a private quarry. I threw all my fire out. That's when we had to use the long-shafted shovel."

Having plenty of water was a vital necessity. "I'd come off the Shed at Hellifield with a full tank of water. And I'd 'appen have 500 gallons out of the tank when I set off from the sidings. I used to stop at Settle to get water. One day I was 'inside' at Settle for something and this Carlisle driver came. He was a character. He'd stopped at Settle for water and he let the train move back. Consequently, when getting water, he'd pulled the darned crane over. There were water all over t'place. I remember saying: 'You blooming idiot'! I did curse 'im! Cos he was stood there on the main line and I was fast inside. I couldn't get out."

The fireman was expected to operate the water-cranes but some drivers would take pity on their mates and would disembark to turn on the water; then the fireman did not have to

"…and down would go the scoop."

clamber off the back of the tender. "We'd arrive at Settle. The driver would stop his engine in a precise place so that when the arm of the crane was swung it would be just right for getting water. The fireman used to scramble over the coals and put the 'water bag' in. We always called it a 'bag'. It was made of leather, I've seen us take on water at Blea Moor when the bag's been frozen so hard that the fireman had to kick it in the hole."

Woe betide the fireman if he did not shut off the water in good time. The alternative was to flood the tender, washing coal and muck down on to the footplate. In normal times, the ever-active firemen kept the footplate clean. "When I wasn't shovelling, I used to sweep up. I don't need to tell you where all the muck went!"

It was hoped to pick up water at Garsdale troughs. The driver, after watching for signs of their approach, would suddenly say: "Gerrit in." And the scoop was lowered. "You had your eye on the water gauge, which was in front of you. As soon as it showed about three-quarters full, you started pulling the scoop out. The drivers wanted to see it filled right up to the top. One would say: 'We could hev got some more in there'. If the tank overflowed, you were in lumber. The fireman couldn't win!"

Among the freight engines stabled at Skipton were "the old Derby 4s." Each had a small tank. "If you had a heavy load, you'd leave Skipton with a full tank and hope to get some more water at Settle, which should then take you to Blea Moor. After that, you thought of the troughs at Garsdale, the highest in the world. You could get some more water at Kirkby Stephen, Appleby and so on."

The water troughs near Garsdale were 'hitty-missy'. A driver who had never missed getting water here used the effective but potentially dangerous practice of pulling out the steam brake. "I can't explain exactly what happened but as you pulled it out, you would see the water in the gauge shoot up a bit. You did this till you got to the end of the trough. But you had to be careful. You could have broken loose."

In times of hard frost, men were sent up to Garsdale troughs to keep them free of ice. A heating system was in operation. The workers slept in the platelayers' cabin and took provisions. "Jimmy Antell and Bob Lund were on that job for weeks on end," I was told by a driver who came to know them well.

Collecting water at Garsdale involved split-second timing. "You had the scoop to wind down into the troughs. A concrete post with an oil lamp was supposed to be a marker at night. Being an oil lamp, the marker had usually gone out. So on a pitch-black night, you counted bridges. One. Two. At the third bridge, the scoop must go in.

"Sometimes, you had followed close behind another train and the trough was still filling up with water. Sometimes, it was frozen up and we had to make a water-stop at Appleby. And sometimes, you'd hardly any water left. The driver got a bit jittery in case we couldn't make Appleby in time."

Wise drivers lowered the water scoop a little in advance of the Garsdale troughs. "I'd give it one or two turns on the wheel and then I wasn't wasting any time. Then I'd put it right down, but as soon as I saw the water gauge in the cab begin to move, I'd ease it back about half a turn. Otherwise, I'd be getting to the end of a trough with the tank getting full. I'd have a job breaking a column of water."

It was possible to get too much water – with messy consequences. "Many a time you'd be getting a tank full before you got half way along a trough and then water was splashing all over the place. If it was on a passenger train, in warm weather, and some passengers had their windows lowered, they got wet. It was the guard's duty to walk down the train to advise them to shut the windows.

"I was very fortunate one day. I had a camera with me. I was after a shot down the valley but it was a hazy day. So I took a picture down the side of the locomotives as we got water at Garsdale. You could see the cylinder taps were spitting and one or two spots of water had come on to the window."

Spirit of the Settle-Carlisle Line

Opposite page – A Sprinter unit approaches Dent, the highest station (photo: British Rail).
Below – No.44767 crosses Ribblehead Viaduct.

HAWES JUNCTION & GARSDALE STATION

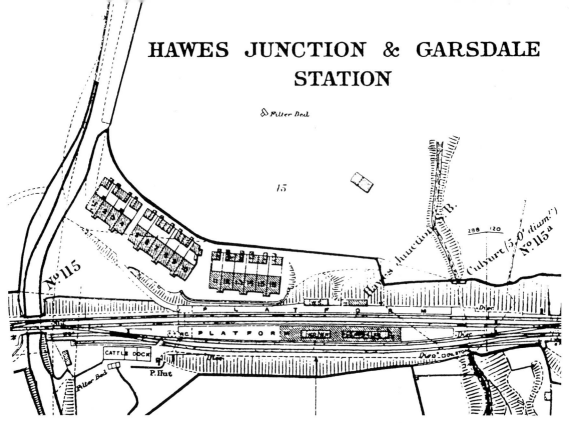

Above – This "Landplan" map is of Garsdale, formerly known as Hawes Junction.
Below – No.4472 Flying Scotsman with a "Cumbrian Mountain Express" takes on water at Garsdale in 1984.

Rain in the Wind

Weather duty, Ribblehead.

THE ELEMENTS conspired to test the footplate men. Tinted leaves falling in autumn might inspire the poet but when they were wet they settled on the tracks on a shadowy stretch like Stainforth Cutting, bringing many a proud train to a standstill, though its wheels continued to spin. "You just had to get yourself out of a predicament like that the best way you could." The ultimate solution was to bring up another locomotive. "They put one behind you to push you up."

The most famous weather story of the Settle-Carlisle concerns the locomotive on the turntable at Garsdale. It was blown round and round, out of control, by a strong wind. Afterwards, a barrier of sleepers was raised round the turntable to cheat the wind. "Same sort o' thing happened to us one day but before

it started to spin, my mate climbed on and shifted it an inch or two, putting it out o' balance. Yon engine stopped itself. We had to send for some assistance from t'station to help us finish pushing it round."

Ribblehead was also a weather station from which coded messages were telephoned hourly to the Air Ministry. A driver relates: "I got to Ribblehead one day and the Station master asked me to put some more coal on the fire. 'I want to see which way the wind's blowing', he said. 'He did that once or twice with me, over the years'."

A driver could tell as he arrived at Ribblehead station what the conditions were likely to be at the viaduct. "With a westerly gale, you got gusts coming right down between Ingleborough and Whernside. It was like

Signal box at Aisgill. Wild Boar Fell lies beyond.

Mossdale Tunnel, noted for its icicles after a cold snap.

somebody blowing down a funnel. I used to say to the fireman: 'Look out, I'm going to knock hell out of the engine'. I always kept going, though. Many a time I've looked back and seen wagon sheets being ripped off and just blown away in the wind like pieces of paper... Then you had to stop at Blea Moor. Men were fastening sheets down. Many a time, you got stopped when you wanted to keep going!"

Wagon sheets were large and heavy. "I've been near Ribblehead viaduct in wild weather when a sheet blew off a wagon. That sheet floated away on the wind like a piece of confetti. It was going uppards, not downwards. I kept thinking – if that lands on a passing car, the driver won't see daylight again for ages!"

Ribblehead Viaduct could be a nightmare in a westerly gale. "The old Class 4 loco. hadn't much cab. If the wind was strong, you got your fire prepared before you got on to the viaduct, and then you and your driver got tucked away in a corner and let the engine chuff across. Three motor cars were blown off a special train at the end of Blea Moor loop."

The severity of the weather at Ribblehead when the wind came from the west is illustrated by the story of the crew of a Derby 4 being worked to Carlisle; they had to "go inside" at Blea Moor. "The rain was torrential. The wind was so strong it was blowing rain into the cab. George and I walked round the framing in the pouring rain and then stood in front of the smoke box outside. We were drier outside the engine than we'd been in the cab!"

In frosty weather, the trackbed on Arten Gill viaduct used to lift. "It was like driving over a corrugated roof. By heck – you hadn't got to go so fast over it. There were always flagmen out when these conditions prevailed. You got stopped and told of the conditions."

In Blea Moor, during the wintry spell of 1963, were icicles as big as... [words failed him]. "They knocked all t'brass handles off t'coaches of t'Carlisle slow as it went through..."

In steam days, there were worse tunnels than Blea Moor. "One was Mossdale, between Garsdale and Hawes, because we used to have to go tender first. It wasn't a very deep tunnel-top. There used to be icicles, stalactites – call 'em what the heck the likes – and as we were coming down they were breaking off at tender-end and dropping on t'footplate."

When dealing with drifts across the line, the driver of a locomotive with a snow plough was expected to open the regulator, increase speed and barge into them. "You had an engine leading and an engine trailing. They were back to back. Each was equipped with a plough, so you could plough one way and plough back again. You would have a brake van in the middle." If the plough did not clear the snow, another "charge" was planned. "Snow used to come up through the footboards and from t'sides; there were sheets to stop it coming from above, but they weren't always effective."

A locomotive inspector who rode with the crew when snow-ploughing was taking place attracted attention because he was so well dressed. "He was new to the district and turned up with a beautiful blue Melton overcoat, smart suit, a Homberg and rubber boots on his feet. Usually, an inspector wore his oldest clothes, with an old donkey jacket and wellingtons."

That Terrible Moor

THE SHAFTS of Blea Moor were equipped with "garlands" as part of the drainage system; water from a garland found its way into a downpipe which was connected with the main drain of the tunnel. After heavy rain, the driver of a steam locomotive might still be soaked while passing under a shaft. He often had his head out of the cab, looking ahead. He tried to avoid doing this in the tunnel, "otherwise, you had a stream of water down the back of your neck!"

Leeds men were the butt of many a joke by the footplate men of Skipton and Hellifield. "There was a smart Leeds feller – I hope he hears about this or reads this; it will serve him reight – who said: 'Nah then, you're working at the third ventilator in the tunnel. I'm going to ride with yer to make sure you don't overshoot it.'

"I said: 'You needn't bother, lad. I'll hit third ventilator spot on wi' t'tender end; will that do thi'? He said: 'You won't see it'. I said: 'You don't knew it all, even if thou does come fra Leeds'. So anyway, we entered the 'ole. He insisted on riding on t'engine. He worn't watching me, but when we got to approaching the second hole my hands were out o' t'cab, feeling for t'watter dropping out of t'ventilator shaft.

"Then when we were half way between sheer and t'next 'un, a feller passed us rolling it out [a passing train emitted a lot of smoke!] so there were nowt visible. I started going slow from thereon, of course. He said: 'We aren't there yet'! I said: 'I knaws; shut thee gob'. 'When I felt t'watter, I was almost on t'point o' stopping – stalling, they call it – and I stopped and said to 'im: 'If thou walks back a yard or two, thou'll find thissen half way under the

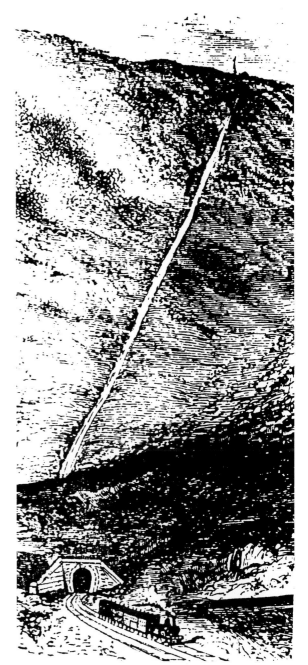

Blea Moor, as pictured in "The Midland Railway," by F.S. Williams.

ventilator.'

"After a quarter of an hour or so, he came back and said: 'Can you see in this murk'? I said: 'Yes'. He said: 'By gow – that's a wonderful asset'. See? I couldn't see through that murk: who could? Nobody!"

The signalman at Blea Moor box cut the hair of visiting railwaymen. "He got quite a bit of custom because crews waited in the box for the arrival of trains from Carlisle; they would change over with the Carlisle men. One evening, just after haytime, I was waiting in the box when I heard a clomping on the steps and into the box came six farmhands. They all had their hair long, like hillbillies. The signalman started cutting their hair and I swept it up to keep the box clean.

Some of the permanent way men and their families lived in cottages the railway company built at the lineside near Blea Moor signal box. It was a lonely spot. A platelayer's wife regarded it as a good day out when she had a trip on the express called Bonnyface. She was taken through to Hawes and was back home an hour or two later. "That woman left her home on one day in the week and at holidaytime." I was told.

A driver who took water and coal to Blea Moor on the Carlisle pick-up said: "The wagon of coal was put off by Blea Moor box and the platelayers shovelled it off."

Bill Davison, a member of the Tunnel Gang for 19 years, was a Methodist local preacher who sometimes took a service at Dent. He carried his bike through Blea Moor tunnel, rode down the dale to Dent Town and returned by the same route. "It was quiet in Blea Moor Tunnel on a Sunday." said Bill.

Jack Dawson, was a member of the Tunnel Gang at Blea Moor who did not see daylight during the working day in winter. "He used to go into the tunnel in the early morning when it was dark and he'd come out in the late afternoon, when it was dark. On so many weeks in the year, he was always in the dark. He got 9s a week extra on his wage and this was known to the men as 'muck money'."

They also served. One of the caterers gets a breath of fresh air.

Lean
and
Hungry

"Sometimes the crews would cook their food – especially bacon and eggs – by resting a cleaned shovel on the edge of the firebox."

ONE OF THE fallacies of the Steam Days is that the footplate men cooked their meals on the fire as the train went happily on its way. In fact, sandwiches were the principal fare. They could be eaten "amang hands" or during a brief lull. A driver who confessed he was not very good at cooking bacon and egg told me: "We used to take potatoes and onions and put 'em at the back of the injector pipe. By the time we got to Blea Moor, there was a lovely smell.

"People imagine you had a great big roaring fire on which you cooked bacon and egg. It's a bit of a myth. If you had a shovel and you put bacon on it and shoved it in the firebox when it was red-hot, your bacon would just go wheww! And your eggs with it!

"Somebody might cook a meal when he'd finished his shunting and had an hour or so in the yard. He'd bring the embers back under the door; then wash the shovel and smear it with a

"Leeds men were posh; they had enamel tea cans; we just had pop bottles wi' tea in."

bit of lard. The bacon was laid in the back of the shovel, which was gently held over what was left of the fire. When he'd turned the bacon, the fat had run down into the shovel-back and all was ready for an egg.

"Personally, I'd rather have sandwiches and a bottle of tea, though I once had a cooked meal in Leeds City Station at 4 o'clock in the morning. When I fired for one driver, we used to work a fish-train. They unloaded fish at Leeds in the early hours of the morning. Sometimes fish would fall between the lines. My driver went round and picked up one or two fresh herrings. He gutted and cleaned them and we baked them on his shovel. They were lovely!"

Leeds men were considered to be posh; they had enamel tea cans. "We just had pop bottles wi' tea in…"

As already stated, railwaymen subsisted on sandwiches. "My wife used to say: 'What are you taking for 'packed-up' today: cheese or an egg'? I used to say: 'Yes'.

"'What's matter wi' t'cheese then'?

"'I'll have cheese'.

"'Oh-what's matter wi' t'egg then'?

"That's how it was. They were just sandwiches, anyway. I had sandwiches every blooming day."

There was no stopping the train to eat. "You had your grub while you were running." On a Derby engine, two pipes through which steam was supplied to the sander formed a loop. "There was just enough room for a bottle of tea; if there wasn't quite enough room – we made it fit! So we kept the tea warm." The owner of the bottle had to remember to loosen the cork or "when it got hot, it would blow its top."

If you were working the Garsdale pick-up or the Hawes pick-up, you might manage a brief spell of mushrooming in a lineside field between signal boxes. At the next box, the man might think: "He's taking his time today." Men on a train going down the Hawes line just before Christmas were known to stop near a berried holly tree and jump off the engine to pick a few sprigs.

Footplate men on the freight trains who had lodged at Carlisle, returned to Leeds with countryside produce – with rabbits or eggs, bought at certain signalboxes. Crosby Garrett was a good place for getting rabbits. "On our way back to Leeds, we'd look out for pairs of rabbits dangling from the railings of the signal box. They were for sale at 2s.6d the pair. The driver would turn to the fireman and say: 'Ay up – he's got some'!"

The fireman dampened down the fire, then leapt off the locomotive and sprinted to the signal box, running up the steps. The signalman had his hands on the bells; he did not see the visitor nor did he want to know anything about him. In those days, everything was strictly point-to-point timing.

"You banged the money down. And you grabbed what you had paid for. Then you were off down the steps, slinging the rabbits over your shoulder as you started to run so that you could catch up with your engine. The driver hadn't stopped. He daren't stop or the guard would book it. The guard was the man with the watch. You threw the rabbits on the footplate and jumped on. Then you got t'shovel because you'd got to catch up. The driver had lost some time – all of two minutes. He had to make it up, not between Crosby Garrett and Aisgill but between Crosby Garrett and t'next box.

"You'd get one decent rabbit and the other would be like a little ferret. The better rabbit had a nice dark, rich liver. It was a good rabbit. The other was a pathetic thing, with a pale and speckled liver. It was not fit to make gravy of…"

A Carlisle guard paid particular attention to the animals in the cattle trucks. "At Appleby, he walked alongside the train to have a look at the cattle. When one beast had fallen, he came up to me – I was getting water – and said: 'We've a cow down. We'll have to take that truck into the dock and reload it. So we put it on the dock'."

The wagon was fairly well back; which meant that when the driver went up, and he hooked off, and they backed into the dock, the train was blocking both main lines. The guard

"A Carlisle guard paid particular attention to the animals in the cattle trucks…"

Above – Crosby Garrett signal box. "On our way back to Leeds, during t'war, when things were rationed, we'd look out for a pair of rabbits dangling from the signal box."

Below – A pause for the crew of No. 75019 on an Engineer's train at Aisgill.

had to attend to the cattle on his own, but there were no problems really.

"I thought: 'He's a long time'. So I went down and there was not a soul about. In a bit, he came back. He was panting. He was one animal short.

"'Noo', he said, 'it ran coon there. I ran after it. I couldn't catch the coo'. He never did get it. So we saw a policeman and said: 'If you see a cow that's running about in Appleby, let the railway know.'

"When it all came out, he'd let them into this pen and somebody had left the gates open; it had got out on to the road. And off it went!"

The trouble with sheep is that they are inclined to run towards the train rather than away from it. It was all right suggesting that the Blea Moor sheep should be provided with a timetable but, as a driver remarked, "What would happen if the train was 'Saturday Only'?" This driver commented that "birds, especially owls, seem to commit suicide by flying straight into the windscreen of a diesel train."

Above – Inspector Gordon of Carlisle and
Kim Malyon on No.46229 at Garsdale.
Bottom – Dent, in the days of regular steam
(R & L Hinson).

In Time of War

An artist's impression of a wartime scene at Warcop station as a tank train arrived via the Settle-Carlisle line. The gun barrels were often removed while the tanks were in transit.

THE OUTBREAK of war in 1939 found the Settle-Carlisle in good order. "They had relayed a lot of the line. I was a fireman at the time. There was a funny stretch in Lazonby Bank where they had experimented with iron sleepers. They were never a success."

The line carried a lot of specials, including troop trains, prisoner of war trains, ambulance trains and iron ore trains. A Hellifield driver recalls going out to relieve the driver of a prisoner of war train at Hellifield. This train was going south. "American troops were in charge of the train. They got out on the platform and stood there with their tommyguns." Another time, he was told to relieve the 10-25 train from Leeds to Glasgow. "I found a soldier on the footplate. He'd placed his gun at the back of the tender. He must have been expecting something…"

Trains conveying tanks to Warcop for training were a familiar sight. "We used to go down to Kirkby Stephen and we picked up conductors to take us on to Warcop and Clifton Moor. I collected one conductor – he was a driver on the railway and also a bookie. He said: 'Jim, will you be on this job tomorrow'? I said: 'I can't really tell –'. It varied from day to day and depended when the specials were running. I asked him why he was interested. He told me he wanted to go hound trailing somewhere in the Lake District, and he could do with a lift to Appleby."

All the stations were blacked out. "A handlamp was placed at the end of the platform to help drivers. If you couldn't see, you could hear. You were accustomed to the sound of viaducts and cuttings and overbridges."

Hellifield was crucial, being the junction at the approach to the Settle-Carlisle line. During the 1939-45 war, there was a "scare." A story circulated that "they" were going to blow up a bridge over the railway. "The police were all round the village for quite a long time." A driver going on duty wearing a new pair of hand-made boots created such a racket in the subway at the station that a jittery auxiliary policeman said he thought he was being approached by a regiment of soldiers.

Even in 1939, there was much military material on the railway. "It was apparent to railwaymen that something was going to happen." The driver of a freight train heading for Carlisle saw a troop train heading south. "Everybody was saying there was going to be an Invasion."

A Hellifield driver who signed on before noon had told his wife to expect him home shortly after 8pm. "I was due out of Carlisle at 6-something." It was wartime, but he had been told that traffic had eased a little. At Long Preston box, the fireman went to sign in for him. He asked the signalman about the situation between here and Carlisle. There was a train standing at every box to Carlisle. "I remember that when we were stopped at Lazonby we were tired and hungry and I just nodded off. The fireman said to me: 'Ay – he's pulled off'. I said: 'Has he? I've got to that state when I'm not bothered'. It had been 'off' nearly a quarter of an hour! I arrived in Carlisle at about 7.30am next day!

"Just before the Second Front [the invasion of Europe] took place, a trainload of jeeps passed me. Americans were sitting in the jeeps and, it being cold, they had the jeep engines running! Those Americans also had the jeep lights on and from one direction there was a blaze of red all the way down the train. The drivers of other trains couldn't reckon it up."

No.5305 drifts into Long Preston for a water stop in July, 1986.

Some Drivers' Yarns

The crew of No.5690 *Leander* take a photo-call at Appleby.

TO HEAR one of the old drivers tell a tale about the line, using a smattering of dialect to emphasise some telling point, was to come close to experiencing the true spirit of those who manned the steam trains on the Settle-Carlisle railway.

A Skipton man was the driver of a No.3 goods engine, heading south from Carlisle on a hot day early in the 1939-45 war. He recalled for me how he stopped at Garsdale and picked up a man with a plausible story who then went to collect a most suspicious parcel.

"We were not doing bad for steam but we were overloaded, which we all were at that time. We had to stop for water at Appleby and Kirkby Stephen. I said to my fireman: 'We'll stop at Garsdale because passenger train (Bonnyface) will have gone from Hawes. My bottle's empty'. He said: 'Are we all right for stopping'? I said: 'Oh, aye – we're bound to be. T'passenger will have gone and it's got to clear Dent Head before they'll let us clear Garsdale. Take your time.'

"We stopped at the island platform. While we were filling our bottles and drinking, this fellow walked round and he had a brief case. He said: 'Fine day, chaps'. I said: 'Aye – and you're getting your share of it.' He said: I'm getting more than my share of it... where are you going to'? 'Skipton'. 'Is Skipton this side of Settle or the other side?' 'Other side. What for'? 'Because the only chance I have of getting a ride is to persuade YOU to take me."

"I asked to see his ticket. He had a day's excursion ticket, Settle to Hawes return. I asked him why he'd missed the train. 'Well', he said, 'I thought I had time to walk it from Hawes to Garsdale.' He had allowed himself an hour and three-quarters. I said: 'Well it worn't enough to start wi'. But secondly, thou's bin calling...' [at public houses] He said he'd had one or two calls.

"I said: 'Oh, well – can ta keep thi gob shut?' He said: 'what do you mean'? I said:

Stainer 8F No.8253 on an Engineer's Train.
"You have a chance to make history today
on a No.8…"

"Exactly what I said. If thou starts blowing it in a club or a pub or anywhere where there's somebody 'at matters, about having a ride on an engine between Garsdale and Settle, two fellows here 'I'll get t'sack'.

"He said he could keep it dark. So he got on t'engine. He shoved his brief case in. He then shoved our lodging basket to each side, then went back where he'd come from and returned wi' a roll o' sacking (a side of bacon).

"We set off. There was Horton pick-up in front of us – that was definite. It stopped at Stainforth and Settle and then it was a toss up if Bentham pick-up had gone or not. We had Hawes pick-up behind us. As we entered the hole [Rise Hill Tunnel], smoke were pouring out: it were one of them days. Me and my fireman had our eyes on 'im. Fireman said afterwards: 'His eyes came out like chapil hat-pegs when we hit this smokebank and went in. I thought he was going to jump off'.

"When we got out, t'other end, he were the colour of a corpse. Blea Moor were worse. And, of course, it's a bit longer. And he was at side where watter spattered in. Anyhow, we got out. We got stopped at Ribblehead. It was nobbut a check; not a real stop. At Stainforth, we got stopped proper. I said: 'We'll be here twenty minutes, owd lad. Thou's nearly time to walk it to Settle'.

"He asked how far it was. I said: 'I've never walked it; I couldn't tell you. I reckon it would take half an hour; but it might not take half an hour wi' that lot'. He said: 'How will I get off at Settle'? I said: 'There ain't no difficulty about that. I will stop. We'll put the water-bag in and when the road is clear I'll set you down on t'muck and I'll see you on the road. Then you'll have to find your own way. But keep your gob shut'.

"I nivver heard owt from that day to this – whether he felled somebody or whether he didn't – but I can imagine him swanking."

Here's a tale heard at Skipton:

"I was on at 5-19am. Well – that were t'train time! I've actually forgot t'loading. I think we'd about 19 o' them things that took iron ore. We were Carlisle next stop, of course. Now to cut a long story short – if I could pass Appleby before Thistle Plaster pick-up left Appleby, I could reach Carlisle in time to be lifted off that engine and go and catch from Durran Hill sidings the 10-15 Birmingham.

"I knew all them lads. They'd stop outside Shed at Skipton for me to drop off so that I wouldn't have so far to walk. One of t'reasons were that whenever I doubleheaded them to Aisgill, I always left them the water at Garsdale troughs. They'd come a bloody long way, hadn't they? In other words, I did my duty.

"I just had a guard. I won't mention his name. He's deeard, though. He worn't well-liked at Skipton. I said: 'Nah then – kick thee brake off'! He said: 'What for'? I said: 'Because I want 10-15 out o' Carlisle'. He said, slowly: 'You want to be careful today'. That's all. He didn't say t'war's ower nor nowt. I said: 'Thee keep thi brake off. I'll do t'rest'. I had to stop at Stainforth because he'd left a brake pinned down. Shows how I were shiftin'.

"Then away we went. We didn't get stopped till we got to Appleby. I did notice, subconsciously, that there were nothing on the up-road. We passed one of the Scots – only one – in Blea Moor Tunnil. The other, seemingly, had been cancelled – unbeknown to me. I went into t'Box at Appleby, to see what we were stopping for and to try and get to knew whether Thistle Plaster had gone.

"The only satisfaction I got out of him was to be told that Thistle Plaster was not running. I said: 'What the hell are we waiting for, then'? He said: 'You're waiting here to see if they can get someone to change ower'. I said: 'Change ower. You get the doings off, lad. We want 10-15 out o' Carlisle'. He said: 'It's cancelled'. I thought: 'There's summat funny here'. Eventually, he let us go. We pulled off – and away we went!

"We were making up for lost time. A train usually runs down into t'Eden Valley. In fact, you used to handbrake a little bit. But not that day, we didn't. 'Back signal' was on at Langwathby. As we were approaching t'outer, he popped a red flag out of t'window—which they did, for it was customary. He shoved his heeard out of t'window and said: 'You're swapping ower'. I said; 'Nivver'.

No.71000 Duke of Gloucester leaving Garsdale northbound, on the Cumbrian Mountain Express.

"Up the Pennine, down the Pennine; up the Pennine, down the Pennine – I thought, heck, we're going to have our money's worth. Anyway, fireman went potty. I said: 'Don't worry, lad; what thou can't do, I can'. Eventually, signalman said: 'He's coming now. When you've changed over, draw up to my up-starter and when the guards have changed over, I'll drop it, and then you can go.' I said: 'OK'.

"So when they come, I looked at Carlisle feller – A Durran Hillman – and I said: 'Eh up, there's summat funny here, owd lad'. He said: 'What'? I said: 'You should be lodging at Leeds, shouldn't you'? He said: 'Yes – but I'm afraid you haven't heard the news'. I said: 'News'? Only news I've heard is four pints for nowt in t'Club at dinner-time'. He said: 'The war's over. Victory over Japan's assured at last'. I said: 'Ohhhh – is there nowt running then?'

"He wanted to know how many trains I'd passed. I said: 'One – I think. And that were t'Scotch in the tunnil. It was a passenger o' some sort, anyway. He said: 'It'd bi t'Scotch. The other one's cancelled. All men working today must be lifted off and get into their own Control area. They'll get a day in lieu for working and they are in double pay'. I said: 'Eh – that's nice. I'd sooner have four bloody pints for nowt, though'.

"He said: 'All right. You've a chance to make history today in a No. 8. It'll be fully fitted with the exception of the first one, which was off at Hellifield. The vacuum's been tried and the strings have been drawn, and you're running, until you require the ejector, with steam brake only'. I said: 'Oh, reighto – how'm I fixed for watter'? He said: 'I'm afraid you'll have to stop at Appleby. I don't think you've got enough to reach the troughs.' That was bad.

"So we stopped at Appleby and we filled

No.60009 Union of South Africa at Aisgill, September, 1985.

A "Class 5" on a down goods, south of Settle.

the tank up. I estimate I lost four minutes between Langwathby and Appleby. We were running under class B timings, which gave us 25 minutes from Appleby to Kirkby Stephen and you wanted 22 minutes from Kirkby Stephen to Aisgill. I took 25 minutes to Aisgill – all t'lot! I were shiftin'.

"You've summat on watching for Garsdale's distant. And whether there's owt on t'railway or there isn't, you've got to watch 'em. Eventually I spotted it. And instead of letting 'em run, like they did do, the regulator came open again… and that was that! We did from Aisgill to Settle Junction in record time.

"I kept looking back at t'guard's brake. It were wobbling about. He couldn't do owt. He could only put his own brake on. He hadn't got t'vacuum brake. He couldn't stop us. I estimated that at various places on the roadway I was doing 85 miles an hour, which was illegal. Those men who can confirm what I did are dead now. One was t'driver who relieved me. And t'other man was his fireman. (It was t'fireman who made the remark: 'By gum, lad – you've travelled! At each signal box that you've past,

chap said: 'This is him'! and next minute you'd gone'!).

"Relief driver said: 'I was sorry to come away misself. But if it's any consolation, I shall be relieved as soon as we get in t'Leeds area, and t'first, most expeditious way home will be mine. Even if I have to get on a bus'!

"As for me, that VJ Day ride was the best trip I ever had…"

The water tower at Settle station.

Historic Pictures of the S-C

Left – A Class 4 moves to be coaled at Hellifield while a Black 5 arrives with a passenger train for Leeds.

Below – BR Class 4MT 4-6-0 No.75048. In the 1960s, a locomotive such as this saw much service on the Settle-Carlisle and gave the footplate crews better weather protection than they had experienced.

MIDLAND RAILWAY, Dec 21st 1900. P. F. 45.

From Hawes Junction   To Settle
Mr Bilcock Inspector

Dear Sir
      As the Pilot Engine No 1310. Was turning
on the Turntable this morning the Wind being so
Strong the Engine Got beyond Control
      the following are the Names Who Was
Called out to Assist Called out by Signalman
time Called out 5.30 am till 6.30 am by Sutton

The message sent from Hawes Junction (now Garsdale) in 1900 when a strong wind spun
a pilot engine out of control on the unguarded turntable.

MIDLAND RAILWAY, 190. P. F. 45.

From   To

Benson   Andrew   Ganger
Fothergill John   Under "
Blades   John   Lab
Brown   James   "
Kindllyside John   Ganger
Thompson   Christhofer Lab

                         Yours truly
                         A Benson

Southern Railway 777 (Sir Lamiel) makes a "run past" at Garsdale with steam to spare.